C000143519

BEST MUM IN THE WORLD

summersdale

BEST MUM IN THE WORLD

Illustrations by Rosie Brooks.

Summersdale Publishers Ltd
46 West Street
Chichester
West Sussex
PO19 1RP
UK

www.summersdale.com

Printed and bound by Tien Wah Press, Singapore

ISBN: 1-84024-555-7
ISBN 13: 978-1-84024-555-4

BEST MUM IN THE WORLD

The strength of motherhood is greater than natural laws.

Barbara Kingsolver

There was never a great man who had not a great mother.

Olive Schreiner

To describe my mother would be to write about a hurricane in its perfect power.

Maya Angelou

If I was damned of body and soul,
I know whose prayers would make
me whole,
Mother o' mine, O mother o' mine.

Rudyard Kipling

My mother's great. She has the major looks. She could stop you from doing anything, through a closed door even, with a single look.

Whoopi Goldberg

When you are a mother, you are never really alone in your thoughts. A mother always has to think twice, once for herself and once for her child.

Sophia Loren

No gift to your mother can ever equal her gift to you – life.

Anonymous

14

[Motherhood is] having someone else to blame when there is a rude smell in the air.

Jane Horrocks

The heart of a mother is a deep abyss at the bottom of which you will always find forgiveness.

Honoré de Balzac

[A] mother is one to whom you hurry when you are troubled.

Emily Dickinson

Life began with waking up and loving my mother's face.

George Eliot

A mother is the truest friend we have, when trials heavy and sudden, fall upon us; when adversity takes the place of prosperity; when friends who rejoice with us in our sunshine desert us; when trouble thickens around us, still will she cling to us.

Washington Irving

Mother is the name for God in the lips and hearts of little children.

William Makepeace Thackeray

*My mother had a slender,
small body, but a large heart –
a heart so large that everybody's
joys found welcome in it, and
hospitable accommodation.*

Mark Twain

Youth fades; love droops;
the leaves of friendship fall;
A mother's secret hope
outlives them all.

Oliver Wendell Holmes

A mother is she who can take the place of all others but whose place no one else can take.

Cardinal Mermillod

*That best academy,
a mother's knee.*

James Russell Lowell

She may scold you for little things,
but never for the big ones.

Harry Truman

God could not be everywhere,
so he created mothers.

Jewish Proverb

A suburban mother's role is to deliver children obstetrically once, and by car forever after.

Peter De Vries

A mother is not a person to lean on but a person to make leaning unnecessary.

Dorothy Canfield Fisher

*Mothers are the most
instinctive philosophers.*

Harriet Beecher Stowe

Any mother could perform the jobs of several air traffic controllers with ease.

Lisa Alther

No painter's brush, nor poet's pen
In justice to her fame
Has ever reached half high enough
To write a mother's name.

Ralph Waldo Emerson

*Motherhood: all love begins
and ends there.*

Robert Browning

The most remarkable thing about my mother is that for thirty years she served the family nothing but leftovers. The original meal has never been found.

Calvin Trillin

If you desire to drain to the dregs the fullest cup of scorn and hatred that a fellow human being can pour out for you, let a young mother hear you call dear baby 'it'.

Jerome K. Jerome

What do girls do who haven't any mothers to help them through their troubles?

Louisa May Alcott

Women know
The way to rear up children (to be just)
They know a simple,
merry, tender knack
Of tying sashes, fitting baby shoes,
And stringing pretty words
that make no sense,
And kissing full sense
into empty words.

Elizabeth Barrett Browning

It is not what you do for your children but what you have taught them to do for themselves that will make them successful human beings.

Ann Landers

Mother's love is peace. It need not be acquired, it need not be deserved.

Erich Fromm

Men make a camp;
a swarm of bees a comb;
Birds make a nest;
a woman makes a home.

Arthur Guiterman

A mother understands what a child does not say.

Anonymous

*Some mothers are kissing mothers
and some are scolding mothers,
but it is love just the same,
and most mothers kiss
and scold together.*

Pearl S. Buck

*So for the mother's
sake the child was dear,
And dearer was the mother
for the child.*

Samuel Taylor Coleridge

If evolution really works, how come mothers only have two hands?

Milton Berle

Biology is the least of what makes someone a mother.

Oprah Winfrey

She never quite leaves her children at home, even when she doesn't take them along.

Margaret Culkin Banning

Motherhood has relaxed me in many ways. You learn to deal with crisis.

Jane Seymour

*All that I am or ever hope to be,
I owe to my angel Mother.*

Abraham Lincoln

Mothers' Day is in honour of the best mother who ever lived – the mother of your heart.

Anna Jarvis

Who ran to help me when I fell,
And would some pretty story tell,
Or kiss the place to make it well?
My mother.

Ann Taylor

Motherhood has a very humanizing effect. Everything gets reduced to essentials.

Meryl Streep

Life is the fruit she longs to hand you,
Ripe on a plate.
And while you live,
Relentlessly she understands you.

Phyllis McGinley

A mother's arms are made of tenderness and children sleep soundly in them.

Victor Hugo

Women are aristocrats, and it is always the mother who makes us feel that we belong to the better sort.

John Lancaster Spalding

*How simple a thing it seems to me
that to know ourselves as
we are, we must know
our mothers' names.*

Alice Walker

I cannot forget my mother. She is my bridge. When I needed to get across, she steadied herself long enough for me to run across safely.

Renita Weems

*The real religion of the world comes
from women much more than from
men – from mothers most of all,
who carry the key of our souls
in their bosoms.*

Oliver Wendell Holmes

There is none,
In all this cold and hollow world,
No fount of deep,
strong, deathless love,
Save that within a mother's heart.

Felicia D. Hemans

Most of all the other beautiful things in life come by twos and threes, by dozens and hundreds. Plenty of roses, stars, sunsets, rainbows, brothers and sisters, aunts and cousins, comrades and friends – but only one mother in the whole world.

Kate Douglas Wiggin

The mother loves her child most divinely, not when she surrounds him with comfort and anticipates his wants, but when she resolutely holds him to the highest standards and is content with nothing less than his best.

Hamilton Wright Mabie

*A man's work is from sun to sun,
but a mother's work is never done.*

Author unknown

*For the hand that rocks the cradle
is the hand that rules the world.*

William Ross Wallace

The tie which links mother and child is of such pure and immaculate strength as to be never violated.

Washington Irving

The mother's heart is the child's school-room.

Henry Ward Beecher

My mother had a great deal of trouble with me, but I think she enjoyed it.

Mark Twain

There was a place in childhood that I remember well,
And there a voice of sweetest tone bright fairy tales did tell.

Samuel Lover

A mother's love is patient and forgiving when all others are forsaking, and it never fails or falters, even though the heart is breaking.

Helen Steiner Rice

Stories first heard at a mother's knee are never wholly forgotten – a little spring that never quite dries up in our journey through scorching years.

Giovanni Ruffini

One of the very few reasons I had any respect for my mother when I was thirteen was because she would reach into the sink with her bare hands – bare hands – and pick up that lethal gunk and drop it into the garbage.

Robert Fulghum

I shall never forget my mother, for it was she who planted and nurtured the first seeds of good within me.

Immanuel Kant

Mother's love grows by giving.

Charles Lamb

89

A little girl, asked where her home was, replied, 'Where mother is.'

Keith L. Brooks

A mother's happiness is like a beacon, lighting up the future but reflected also on the past in the guise of fond memories.

Honoré de Balzac

Every beetle is a gazelle in the eyes of its mother.

Moorish proverb

I remember my mother's prayers and they have always followed me. They have clung to me all my life.

Abraham Lincoln

www.summersdale.com